# EVERYDAY CODING __

## FOLLOWING INSTRUCTIONS

### Using Control

## Elizabeth Schmermund

Cavendish
Square
New York

Published in 2018 by Cavendish Square Publishing, LLC
243 5th Avenue, Suite 136, New York, NY 10016

Copyright © 2018 by Cavendish Square Publishing, LLC

First Edition

Cataloging-in-Publication Data

Names: Schmermund, Elizabeth.
Title: Following instructions: using control / Elizabeth Schmermund.
Description: New York : Cavendish Square, 2018. | Series: Everyday coding | Includes bibliographical references and index. | Audience: Grades 2-6.
Identifiers: ISBN 9781502629890 (library bound) | ISBN 9781502629876 (pbk.) | ISBN 9781502629883 (6 pack) | ISBN 9781502629906 (ebook)
Subjects: LCSH: Computer programming--Juvenile literature.
Classification: LCC QA76.6 S36 2018 | DDC 005.1--dc23

Editorial Director: David McNamara
Editor: Caitlyn Miller
Copy Editor: Nathan Heidelberger
Associate Art Director: Amy Greenan
Designer: Christina Shults
Production Coordinator: Karol Szymczuk
Photo Research: J8 Media

The photographs in this book are used by permission and through the courtesy of:
Front cover, Hero Images/Getty Images; p. 4 Hurst Photo/Shutterstock.com; p. 8 Kirill Smirnov/Shutterstock.com; p. 11 Catalin Petolea/Shutterstock.com; p. 12 Carballo/Shutterstock.com; p. 15 Rubberball/Getty Images; p. 16 Light Field Studios/Shutterstock.com; p. 18 Monkey Business Images/Shutterstock.com; p. 19 (left) JGI/Tom Grill/Blend Images/Getty Images, (right) Rawpixel.com/Shutterstock.com; p. 20 Mady70/Shutterstock.com; p. 22, Theerapong28/Shutterstock.com; p. 23 Kpatyhka/Shutterstock.com; p. 24 Elise Peterson, own work/File: Leatherback Turtle eggs hatching at Eagle Beach, Aruba.jpg/Wikimedia Commons; p. 25 FamVeld/Shutterstock.com; p. 26 Daniel Verrier/EyeEm/Getty Images; p. 27 Rawpixel.com/Shutterstock.

Printed in the United States of America

# TABLE OF CONTENTS __

# Rules and Order

To turn on a light, you might flip a light switch. You know exactly what will happen next. The light will come on. There's something just like this in computer coding to tell a computer what to do in different situations. But what is computer coding? Basically, coding just means writing up a set of instructions that a computer must follow. **Code** must be written in a certain way.

*Opposite:* Flipping a light switch leads to a light turning on or off. A computer needs code to tell it how to react to your actions.

Otherwise, computers can't understand or follow it. A computer works differently than a human mind. We might be able to guess what the next step in a problem might be. We can also skip steps if we think they aren't needed. Computers cannot do either of these things. This is why it is so important for code to be written clearly.

Computer code says which step comes first. It says what comes next, too. Code tells the computer what it must do in a situation. Using code that tells a computer what to do and in what **order** is called **control**. Coders use what they call **control structures** to make it happen.

# CHAPTER 01

# A Closer Look at Using Control

Every day, you make many choices. If it is raining, you might have indoor recess. If it is sunny, you go outside instead. Deciding where to have recess depends on the weather. It is a choice that you and your teachers think through. A computer **program** couldn't make a decision like that by itself. It needs to have the right code. The **programmer** who invented a recess program would need to include code that talks about the weather.

Every day you make decisions. One is deciding whether or not to play outside if the weather is bad.

Computer programmers who want a computer to act in a certain way first need to build a set of instructions. These instructions are called **algorithms**. Think of an algorithm as a set of instructions that must be used to solve a particular problem. You could follow an algorithm to take a quiz. First, you put your name at the top of your paper. Next, you answer question one. Then, you answer the rest of the questions. Finally, you turn in your quiz.

An algorithm always solves a problem. You can also think of an algorithm like a recipe. You have to follow the steps of the recipe in order.

This means that step two must follow step one and so on. This is the same way a coder must use algorithms.

Code is built upon these rules, or algorithms. Code is made up of both numbers and letters. If you change the order of these numbers and letters, the instructions for the program change. That can make it difficult for the program and the computer to figure out what to do. So programmers must build the order, called control, into their code.

There are many types of control structures that decide the order to follow. We'll talk about three important ones. **Conditionals** are the first we'll talk about. Think of choosing where to go for recess. If it is sunny, you go outside. The weather is a **condition**. Is it rainy? Then you'll skip going outside. Is it sunny? Then the "sunny" condition is met. You get to go outside! Conditionals are instructions that are followed if certain conditions are met.

**Loops** are another control structure. These are instructions that can be repeated. This is like when you are hungry. You eat a meal when you are hungry. As you eat, you think about if you are full. You keep eating if you decide you are not yet full. Eating is a loop that stops when you are full.

Finally, there are **event handlers**. These are instructions that can be followed only if a certain event (such as clicking a mouse) has taken place. This is exactly like flipping a light switch. The light is not going to turn on by itself. You must flip the switch.

If you look at code, you'll often see control structures working together.

## Mixing It Up

The three basic control structures can be mixed together and repeated. This helps a computer to correctly follow its instructions. Sometimes the control structures are very simple. Sometimes they are **complex**. But they all make the instructions easier for the computer to follow.

# CHAPTER 02

# Using Control in Everyday Life

**W**e use algorithms in our everyday lives. Remember, an algorithm is a list of steps that a computer must follow to solve a particular problem. Think of yourself as a computer. When you wake up in the morning, you have to solve the problem of getting ready for school. In order to solve this problem, you know you have many **tasks** to complete. Some of them must be

*Opposite:* Algorithms are like the plans we make for the day as soon as we wake up.

completed in order. For example, you don't want to put on your new school clothes before taking your shower! That would be a waste of time. Instead, you come up with this list:

- Turn off the alarm.

- Take a shower.

- Get changed for school.

- Eat breakfast.

- Get your backpack ready.

- Make it to the bus stop on time.

This is a simple algorithm that you must follow in order to get to school on time. Notice that you can't switch around different tasks. For example,

One of the tasks you complete to get ready every morning is brushing your teeth. You must decide on an order for doing all the tasks.

getting to the bus on time must be the last step, and turning off the alarm must be the first step.

Algorithms in real life—and in computer programming—can be much more complex. This is where control structures are needed. Let's look

Organizing your backpack requires an algorithm.

at a more complex algorithm that makes use of control structures:

- Turn off the alarm.

- Get out of bed.

- Brush teeth.

- Take a shower.

- Get changed for school.

- Eat breakfast.

- Ask yourself: Did I complete all of my homework I need for today?

  » If yes, put completed homework and books in your backpack.

  » If no, finish homework after breakfast.

- Ask yourself: Is my backpack already packed?

  » If it is, then you can relax for fifteen minutes.

  » If it isn't, then you should get your backpack ready.

- Make it to the bus stop on time.

This is an example of an algorithm that uses conditionals. The conditionals are the questions

Using conditionals like Boolean logic can help you make it to the school bus on time.

# Boolean Logic

**Boolean logic** is an important part of conditionals. Boolean logic is like a true or false question. If a condition is true, then the computer will go to the next step of an instruction. If it is false, then the computer will go to a different step.

Control structures are what help you decide in what order to complete tasks.

you asked yourself. Only if you have already completed your homework will you be able to get your backpack ready. Then, only if you have already done your homework and gotten your backpack ready will you be able to relax for fifteen minutes before the bus comes. Here, the algorithm is the set of steps to get ready for the day. And the control structures are the decisions you make about what you'll do. The control structures help you decide the order of your tasks. The order is what we call control.

# CHAPTER 03

# Bringing It All Together

Imagine you are sitting on your couch watching TV. You can't quite hear what the characters in the show are saying. You pick up your remote. You push the up arrow on the volume button. The TV gets louder.

This is a great example of an event handler. Remember that an event handler is a control structure. You pushed a button on the remote.

*Opposite:* Pressing a button on your remote control is like an event handler in coding.

The TV responded just how you wanted it to. Computers are the same. They need programming to tell them how to respond when you click your mouse. The event handler is what does this job.

Think about the last time you played a computer game. Maybe the game required you to click a mouse. Maybe it involved the directional arrows on your keyboard. You might have even typed in the letters of your name for a high score. The computer knew how to respond to these actions. It knew because of control and control structures.

A TV handles events, just as a computer does.

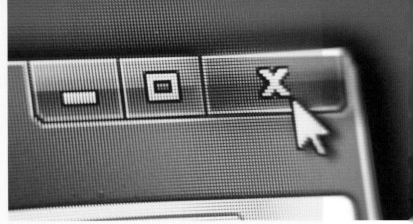

Another example of an event handler is clicking a button in a computer dialog box.

# Understanding Event Handlers

Event handling happens behind the scenes. You probably take it for granted that clicking on an X will close a file. But the computer programmer who wrote the game didn't. He or she wrote code to tell the computer how to handle every condition. This is why control structures are so important.

Imagine you are building a computer game in which you must bring a baby sea turtle to the ocean for the first time.

You can use coding to create computer games. Maybe you are developing a computer game with a baby sea turtle as its central character. The game starts when the baby turtle hatches in the sand. To win the game, the player has to direct the turtle to the sea. There he will meet up with his mother and siblings. You have the idea for the game set. Now you have to create your algorithm. To do this, you have to break down the instructions that you want your computer to follow. These steps will tell the baby turtle how to move.

You come up with the following basic algorithm:

- The baby turtle hatches in the sand.

- It begins walking to the sea.

- It goes into the water and begins to swim.

- It finds its mother and siblings.

A basic algorithm would be the set of instructions that turtle would follow to safely arrive at the ocean.

Following your algorithm means this baby turtle arrived safely!

But this wouldn't make a very exciting game. You have to add in control structures to give the player different choices. You could choose the route the turtle walks. Does the baby turtle turn left or turn right? These kinds of choices make the game interesting. You can now take this very basic algorithm and add in conditionals, loops, or

Computers don't make choices on their own. They need to follow instructions written by coders.

event handlers. The choices the player makes will win or lose them the game.

Computers can't make choices on their own. That's why control is such a big part of computer code. It's a big part of games and other programs. And you use it in your life every day!

# GLOSSARY

**algorithm**  A set of rules or instructions. Computers follow an algorithm to carry out a task or reach a solution.

**Boolean logic**  A true/false question for a computer.

**code**  Instructions that tell a computer how to carry out certain tasks.

**complex**  Complicated.

**condition**  The way something is, or something that must happen before something else can happen.

**conditionals**  Directions that a computer follows only if certain conditions are met.

**control**  The order in which certain instructions must be followed by a computer.

**control structures**  The parts of code that make decisions about the order of steps followed.

**event handler**  Instructions that are carried out only following a certain event, such as the click of a mouse.

**loops**  Instructions that are repeated over and over or until a condition is met.

**order**  The position of something in relation to other things.

**program**  Computer instructions that accomplish a task. Some examples are Microsoft Word and Minecraft.

**programmers**  People who write computer programs.

**task**  A piece of work to be done.

# FIND OUT MORE

**Books**

Bueno, Carlos. *Lauren Ipsum: A Story About Computer Science and Other Improbable Things*. San Francisco: No Starch Press, 2014.

Lyons, Heather, and Elizabeth Tweedale. *Algorithms and Bugs*. Kids Get Coding. London, UK: Wayland, 2017.

**Websites**

**Codecademy**

https://www.codecademy.com

Codecademy is a free website that teaches you to code.

**Code Studio**

http://studio.code.org

Code.org offers free lessons and online courses.

# INDEX

Page numbers in **boldface** are illustrations.

# MEET THE AUTHOR

**Elizabeth Schmermund** is a writer, scholar, and editor who lives with her family in New York. She enjoys writing books for students of all ages. Every day, she tries to balance creative thinking and following instructions.